Psychicbread

Mark Gwynne Jones

The Globe
ock 2004

route

Mark Gwynne Jones

Mark Gwynne Jones is a poet whose surrealistic stories and Tolkeinesque tales are delivered in a manner akin to theatre. You have before you a bard, a busker and storyteller. His black humour and twists and turns of narrative make him a favourite in venues where most poets can only dream of surviving, let alone subduing the crowd to an attentive hush. Drawing on an ancient tradition his captivating and slightly mad, mind altering poems tackle the complexities of our changing world with a beautiful and savage humour. He lives in Derbyshire.

First Published in 2003 by Route
School Lane, Glasshoughton, West Yorks, WF10 4QH
e-mail: books@route-online.com

ISBN: 1 901927 20 2

Cover Photos:© Kevin Reynolds

Cover Design: Andy Campbell

Editor: Ian Daley

The right of Mark Gwynne Jones to be identified as the Author of the
Work has been asserted in accordance with the Copyright, Designs and
Patents Act 1988.

A BIG Thanx 2: Louise and Sam, Andy Postman, John Gill, Josephine
Abbots, Pam Hodges, Matt Szabo, Dylan, Ian Daley, James Gilligan, Roger
Green, Paul Lyalls, Martin Newell, John Cooper Clarke, John Hegley, Dean
Smith, Lemn Sissay, Paul Beasley, Andy Lawrence, Alex Stienitz, John
Stephen, Mike and San Orme, Keith Connock, Richard Walker, Amanda,
Chris Skripek, Carl Hodgkinson, Deb Rose, Jay Schaffe, John Thorne, Paul
Hopkinson, Mick Twelves, Lee Kerr, W. H. Davies, Euan Read and most of
all, my family.

Some of these poems (namely: *The Natterjack Toad*; *It's Only Water* and *The
Birmingham 666*) were first published by *Last Gasp Records* (Skiff 1995).
Others were adapted for film by the production company Itoeye. In 1999,
Carlton TV featured the film-poem *It's Only Water*. The film-poems can be
viewed from the CD at the back of the book, which also features 45 mins.
of Psychicbread audio.

Printed by Bookmarque Ltd, Croydon, Surrey

CD Mastering and Duplication by Clipstore, Leeds

A catalogue for this book is available from the British Library

Full details of the Route programme of books
can be found on our website
www.route-online.com

Route is an imprint of YAC, a registered charity No 1007443

All Rights Reserved

YAC is supported by
Arts Council of England, Wakefield MDC, West Yorkshire Grants

For Beatrice and Peter Gwynne

(i) Aunty, Uncle and the Whole Kebab

A Voice

I never saw hide nor hair,
but the shadow of its wings
crossed the lane and climbed the wall
with supernatural strength.

I never heard the cry of the bird,
but felt beneath my feet
something coursing through the earth
and singing in our sleep…

Blood, Fish and Bones

She said:
'Sex only happens inside your head.
    And our arms and legs are
        feckless flesh, groping.
            Like…
    zombies groping trying to find
        the light that once
            shone inside.'

She was always hot for rough and tumble,
the custard on my rhubarb crumble.
She was blonde, sweet,
go-all-gooey-on-a-lick-of-heat.
So whilst her charms did surely glow
she was right - *they never made the rhubarb grow.*
Something else did that…

planet Earth in a Gucci dress
curvaceous on a pair of legs
eternal muse at once made flesh
and her eyes were laughing when she said:

'Sex only happens inside your mind
and your dangling bits are hard to find…'

I said: 'No they're not!
Sex only happens inside my head
'cos my dangling bits, thank you very much,
are all in dead-end jobs.
Doing holes in the doughnut shop,
planting seeds in a Petri dish.
Have you seen what's grown inside our 'fridge?

'It's a culture
where the feeling rots
and a puzzle:
is the light really off when you close the door?'

Her talk was over marmalade
to let me see but never touch
the flesh behind her ridicule
or down inside her citrus love.

She said:
'Sex only happens inside your dreams
                    and they twist and snarl
                            with growing pains.
And your passion for that physical thing
                is really
                        the yearning
of body and mind and soul to be one.'

She was planet Earth in a Gucci dress
curvaceous on a pair of legs
eternal bliss at 3 o'clock
and the light that once
 never stopped.

Alien Rave

In the spoil heaps of an old lead mine,
abandoned long ago,
was a gathering of aliens
for a freaky all night show.

Their painted ships and chariots
arrived in clouds of dust
for an intergalactic rendezvous
and some time to readjust.

And the crew looked well…Neolithic
kinda' *spacey-far-out-man*!
Breathing fire and fantasy
and danger in the land. However,

all was seen by a boy in the trees
who ran to the *Jug and Glass*;
hammering down moonlit lanes
to burst inside and gasp:

'…Da…Da
I've seen 'em Da!
I've seen 'em with me eyes!
Spaceships… Fire… Aliens…'

His father Bill, with his brain in beer,
stumbled off his stool:
'If there's any chuffin' aliens…
I'll frate em….With me tool!

'D'year that Alf? Aliens b' old lead mine.
What dos mek o' that?'
His friend just slurred *'We'll 'ave 'em.*
We'll go up there and we'll 'ave 'em!'
And drooled upon his lap.

And so it was, on a gallon of ale
they drove up to the scene
where before them lay, between heaps of clay,
Breughl's nightmare dream.

The skies were like a fiery dome
crazed with veins of colour
throbbing sexual overtones
to the beat of a heartless hammer.

And there they were - a thousand freaks
freaking out together.
Aliens on planet Earth
come to take their pleasure.

Medusa heads with tentacles
silhouetted by the light
writhed their bodies around the sound
rumbling in the night.

And Bill stood like one repulsed
and said to his mate amazed:
'Aliens!? Aliens!? Aye thee are!
Thee fuckin' 'ippies at a Rave!'

He hurled abuse, slobbered scorn,
and even showed his tool…
Until in the crowd, there he saw
someone that they knew!

It was his daughter – Carol,
freaking out to the helter-skelter-rhythm.
Her spirit flying way above
a life of small derision.

But the word was out on telegraph.
The police were inundated.
Receiving calls from one and all, who
collectively had stated:

'They're takin' drugs in the woods,
dancing round a fire,
having fun whilst we're at work.
String them up with wire!

'They're takin' drugs in the woods,
abducting local youth.
Transmitting loud repetitive sound,
a distortion of the truth, Officer!'

We reasonably believe that 10 or more persons are attending a
gathering to which section 63 of the Criminal Justice and Public
Order Act applies. We hereby demand that all persons leave the
area immediately. If you fail to do so, you will be detained.

Yes, the plug was pulled at the old lead mine.
The spaceships were impounded.
Busses, trucks and caravans
permanently grounded.

And the crusties, freaks and ravers
were rounded up and charged
with perverting all that's twisted
and loosing mind-at-large. However,

all was seen by a boy in the trees.
Who could not now decide
if it wasn't those in power on planet Earth,
who were aliens in disguise.

Aunty, Uncle and the Whole Kebab

My family are really clever.
They make nuclear bombs,
subaquatic death machines
and hyperactive guns.
They know how to make the world
a safer place to be…
and so at night I rest in peace
in the *arms* of the family.

My family are really clever
building cuckoo-clocks,
theorising deities
and why the monkey drops.
Through laws of quantum physics
our feet don't touch the ground.
Once we knew the world was flat
but now we know it's round
here, somewhere…

'Ere what you on about?
My family is really clever.
They've made lots of dosh
in sexy gear that makes you want
more than what you've got.'

My family think that I'm a nutter!
But I don't know why.
I read good books, say my prayers
and even wear a tie.
Perhaps it's because they caught me once
pulling faces in the park.
I had this girl in stitches there…
'twas her ears that came apart!

My family, who are really clever,
think that I'm a freak
because I like to lose myself
in feeling for feeling's sake.
They burst in here with clubs and guns
screaming *be objective!*
But I just can't keep from falling between
the lines of their perspective.

And yet, my family are *really* clever.
If only we could realise
the beauty of
            unfettered love
that lies behind our eyes.
For in the spaces of our ignorance,
immeasurable and dark,
are worlds within worlds of intelligence
that beat with a human heart.

Asleep Upstairs

From darkening skies we shrank
to broken doors,
hoping one would give
somewhere dry
to stay.

One did.
A drunken hall
that spoke in breaths of love and pain
staggered over piles of rubble
and telephone books,
then showed me the rooms of its
broken home.

Through missing slats you
                    watch the dirt
shift and crack beneath my feet.
'What's it like?' you ask.

My answer is to help you in
and together we explore
the ground floor:

cupboards
hungry for food;
taps choked with thirst and
faithfully waiting a master's return
an armchair rots to the kitchen floor.

You say: 'This'll do.'
But I'm not sure
and start   to climb   the stairs

On the landing there are three
doors, one slightly
ajar. With a touch it opens.
And in this empty house,
this house whose walls absorbed
the screams and thoughts of generations past,

signs of recent life
shock me:

a chair
pulled to the fireside;
cans of beer and candle-burnt
pieces of foil;

salami hangs from the chimneybreast
and there in a bed of hessian sacks
a body sleeps. A long sleep.

For afraid
       to wake
the bricks and mortar,
we crept outside to face the rain.
And *his* face, drawn and pale
beneath a hank of matted hair,
continues to lie

asleep upstairs in an empty house.

(ii) The Breezeblock Waltz

The Natterjack Toad

'Twas either spellbound or mesmerised
the Natterjack Toad - with eyes
like glass - unblinking.
No twitch of the tongue could tell
whether or not the toad was even thinking!

There it lay,
staring at the sky.
Day
   after day
as if waiting for a fly...
But, the Natterjack Toad was in no hurry. No.
She was stuck to the road by a passing lorry!

Yes,
the Natterjack Toad would never go far.
A fact confirmed by the 4x4 Mitsubishi
               with fuel injection
               powered steering
               digital radio
               alloys
and an LPG conversion
               just to show
             how much you care.

All Tanked Up!

I want to drive a Sherman Tank
down to the shops and maybe the bank
to buy some bread and a can of beans.
I'd park on top of Mrs Muldean's people carrier:
a Ford Galaxy in sexy purple,
fucked beneath my lusty turtle!

I want to drive a Sherman Tank
at six o'clock when the roads are jammed.
With my head through the turret
and the radio on
I'd be crushing the cars one by one.
'Cos you might have got a brand new Porsche
or something bigger like a 4x4
but the roads are full
the roads are blocked
and a Sherman Tank can drive on top!

I want to drive a Sherman Tank
with the supergun fully cranked
and the girls gazing up in awe.
Never again would I be ignored, no!
Sat astride that giant tool,
whistling the tune to Battle of the Bulge.
The girls would implode in fits of goo
as I gave them a wink and rumbled through.

I want to drive a Sherman Tank
to demonstrate my decadence.
Out along the Boulevard
I'd make boy racers think their cars
silly by comparison.
And if anyone *dared* to overtake
I'd turn the supergun and wait

until they were 15 miles up the road
(laughing at their turtle jokes)
before the punch line made them groan,
in a burning wreck of twisted chrome.

Yes I want to drive a Sherman Tank
'cos knives and clubs make me pant and
shake and
      sweat with
            fear
and stabbing someone face to face is
hate
     full
       horror
bull-at-a-gate primitive
compared to the executive action of a 77mm missile.
Road rage, eh!? It'd be so much easier in a Sherman Tank.

And eventually when the public twig
and Sherman Tanks are really big
and every trip to the shop and back
rattles and clanks on caterpillar tracks,
I'll leave them to their earthbound mess,
take to the air in a Harrier Jet
and enjoying the space of our heavenly dome
feel like the first
        car on the road…
                car on the road…
             car on the road…

The Breezeblock Waltz (pt.1)

Down the boulevard
faces and forces were fixed like wax
and the pavement was crawling
to carry them back and forth.
           Back and forth.
The people never knew their course,
but the pavement did.
And though littered with crisp packets, dog-ends
and bubblegum,
she carried those waxworks without complaint
around the town and to their fate.

But the web stretches far and wide,
and fate can change and change her mind.
Her laughter says: *You're space made flesh…*
remember… it is good to forget!
She wears the evening like a hat,
the wide brim hiding her face in shadow.
Look! Can you see where she looks?
For sometimes when she turns her head
and the smoke from her mouth evaporates,
you'll see the distant Pleiades
and the subject of their gaze.

And once, when the night was still,
a gust in the street made me stop.
It tore the pavement's pages loose
and for a moment, in the whirling
of their waltz, I did forget.
And then each leaf was laid again.

Helical Staircase

'Is this déjà vu…
or have I been here before?'
said the admin. clerk on his way to work.

'Is this that experience where
one side of the brain is slow tomato ketchup
pounded by a boy
onto the chips and peas of realisation,
or have I been here before?'
said the drunk in the cafe
to the lavatory door.

The helical staircase is made of glass
and beneath our feet we see our passing selves.

'Do you come here often?' she said.
And her voice hung
like a jet plane
scoring a line on the dome of the sky.
'If it cracks we're free…' said I.
And it made me think of the lost balloon.
It made me dream of the face
of the moon we never see.
And she said 'What do you mean:
if it cracks we're free?'

The helical staircase is made of stars,
DNA and water that twists
and turns
            round
and down
            the drain.
Wanting out
but returning as rain.
As souls return, again and again.

The clown, the judge, the terminally ill
daddy inside the eyes of the girl,
the bank clerk thumbing endless notes,
the turtles keeping you afloat,
is this déjà vu?
is this déjà vu?
is this…that experience, where
one side of the brain is slow tomato ketchup
pounded by a boy
onto the chip…

or have I been here before?

Orange Girl

I fell in love with an orange girl
her hair plutonium blonde.
At night she slept on a solar bed
until her skin was bronze.

More than bronze, it was orange.
She was orange,
              radiating heat.
Beside her other girls were dull,
cold and incomplete.

I fell in love with an orange girl
bright as marmalade.
At night she slept on a solar bed
and dreamt in vivid grey…

Dreams of love for who she was
instead of how she looked,
but in the humdrum morning rush
the dream it was forgot.

She wore Chanel, a vacant air,
the poise of *Harpers and Queen*;
I fell in love with a girl who read
enlightened magazines.

The Perfect Man, A Ten Point Plan
To Bulimia and Beyond…
the *Fresher, Thinner You* was found
singing down the john.

I fell in love with a girl who was
more than a day-glow pink.
Even marching Protestants
would shield their eyes and blink.

She was Three Mile Island, the after glow,
a lobster boiled alive,
rescued from the cooking pot
and dressed in Calvin Klein.

I fell in love with an orange girl,
she was the planet Mars,
tripping round electric suns
in a hire purchase car.

I bought her from the beauty store
where beauty is exchanged,
then took her out to show the world
and put my friends to shame.

I fell in love with a girl who freaked
for the DJ's helium love.
How you should have seen her dance
upstairs at the Paradise Club!

Voluminous and luminous
her silicone boobs did bounce
like two Belisha beacons
that held me in a trance.

I fell in love with an orange girl
bright as marmalade.
At night she slept on a solar bed
and dreamt in vivid grey…

Dreams of being sold a lie
by MTV and Vogue,
a vision of perfection
that left her feeling old, bulimic, suffering from melanoma
and decidedly…orange.

Stop the Week

When Monday morning starts to crawl
down the road and up your hall
grab it by the throat and squeeze,
slap its face and please - hold its head
inside a sink. Turn the taps and let it drink
until you think: Monday morning
can drink no more.

Then wait 10 minutes, to be perfectly sure.

Stop the week
cease the wheel
spinning round beneath our heels

Turn your Volvo
in the road
and let the traffic mount in droves

Pull the plug
on television
parliament, a power station

and dance,
to the sound of the earth
breathing sighs of relief.

Somebody, please, stop the week.

When Monday morning starts to heave
down your neck a putrid wheeze
and whispers dead lines in your ear, like:
'C'mon, wake up, its time to wreck the day!'

What is this life if, full of care,
we have no time to stand and stare?

Somebody pull the plug
Somebody pull the plug
Somebody somebody somebody please

Grab the clock
by its hands
and lead it out across the Strand

Take time out
and put it in
a city council wheelie bin!

And dance, dance, dance
to the sound of the earth
breathing sighs of relief.

Somebody, please, stop the week.

(iii) Omens in Bloom

The Birmingham 666

And crossing over to the other side
He took them to a high and sacred place.
And there he spoke of many things
Concerning the turning of one's face
And of the peace it eventually brings.
And later he spoke, saying:

'Beware the digits of the Devil
For they *are* human digits.
I say to you beware
The number of the Beast:
Dial it upside down
And you'll be talking to the police!'

And the crowd saw what he was saying,
And knew that it was good.

Omens in Bloom

I thought I heard the postman
so I went to get the mail,
but all I found was a crumpled note
hanging from a nail. It said:

*'Don't be alarmed if the grass turns yellow and
some birds fall from the sky. There's dioxins in the water
but the levels aren't that high...'*

The rest was getting hard to read.
On and on it went,
so I had a cup of tea
and wondered what it meant.

At noon sometimes, as if from a dream,
I wake to find myself
naked, alive, here inside
a body of mortal health.

And then it's like a lightning strike
I don't know who I am.
The telephone rings. I pick it up.
It's the double glazing man:

'Mr Jones?.. You'll be pleased to know
that you've been selected
for a special, once-in-a-lifetime
double-glazing discount bonanza!'

My god of billions all at sea...
Hiya boys! I'm the Chosen One.
It was written all for me. Jesus Christ!
Mohammed... Buddha,
the Devil-all-in-one.
A sense of purpose was given me
by the double glazing man.

And from that moment, everywhere,
omens did emerge,
from chimney-pots and cups of tea
and in between our words.

There was meaning in a layer of dust
beneath my mother's chair,
but truly what that meaning was
hid behind our fear.

And I could see all sorts of things
just staring at the moon:
a lady looking round in horror
at this ball of blue.

Newspapers blowing down the road
could tell you last week's scam;
but the dust inside my mouth couldn't lie
of dryness in the land.

Hmm…Hailstones in the height of June
and an open car at 4;
a path where once there was a stream
and water runs no more.

These were things that puzzled me.
I said so in the street.
I shouted from the Town Hall steps
what *do* these omens mean?

What does the river symbolise
when it runs from brown to yellow?
And fish that float upon their backs
mouth a wordless memo?

I shouted from the Town Hall steps
but answer came there none
until the police arrested me
and took me in a van.

They said I shouldn't *ask* such things
and: 'How is your wife
                    …these days?'
They said I shouldn't *see* such things
and dowsed me with their sprays.

They left me in a layby
naked and confused
to walk home barefoot 50 miles
logically abused.

On arriving home there was a note
nailed to the door:
a repossession order
from a bank in Singapore.

There was someone in my kitchen
eating all the cheese.
I watched him from the garden,
In a double-glazing-frieze.

And from that moment, everywhere,
I recognised my folly.
A loaf of bread is a loaf of bread
a brolly *is* a brolly.

And if I see what would have been
a portent or a sign:
a farmer in his underpants
shouting at the sky,
or perhaps a hurricane forecast for the world,
I think of purple lingerie

and watch the weather   girl.

Season of mists...

Season of mists and magical fungus,
Brother and guide to the Abraham Heights,
Pull from the earth its psychic juices
In fruiting bodies that push for the light.

Ah season of mists and magic mushrooms
And strangers worrying the bleating sheep,
And farmers advising *Mind it Boyo!*
Between the brook and burning leaf,
Where the drowsy wasp and dead can speak
Of cracks in the world at the end of time,
Where the gates are tied with bailer twine.

It was there they walked with heads hung low
In search of heaven between the grass.
Both 'shrooms and steeples point to the stars!
Some they ate and some they bagged.

Ah season of mists and magic mushrooms,
The skies were full of bleating sheep
And farmers advising *Come by! Come by!*
To a puzzled dog that sits beneath.
Where the babbling tongue of the water speaks:
Old Mother Hubbard went to the cupboard...

Where is reason now?
Yes, where is that slippery fish?
Thrashing on a plate, perhaps,
                Gasping for its breath.
Mouthing words we cannot hear,
Like a tickled trout.
Round and round the microwave.
                Shall we let it out?

Ah season of mists and magic mushrooms,
Flocks of sheep are now calling my name:
*Maaaark...Maaaark...*a heavenly chorus
Between what's real and what's insane.
Where public, police and priest complain
Of cracks in the world at the end of time,
Where the gates are tied with bailer twine.

Plasticman

I knew a man
who lived within
a disposable plastic Sainsbury's bin
bag.
The whole affair was very sad
he was a plastic man
he was a plastic man

A plastic man will last forever
with a plastic mac
in the clement weather
of an indoor shopping superstore.
No he never steps outside the door.
He's a lazy, hazy, instant gravy
polymer daisy plastic man
he's a plastic man

Plastic man loves to spend
on plastic goods that never end.
He's got a plastic car, a plastic life
a plastic lover and a plastic wife
he's a plastic man
he's a plastic man

Intercourse and Super Bowl,
does them both by remote control.
Loves to watch and eat the telly
loves to watch and eat the telly!?
believe me when you see his belly.
He's a rubbery, blubbery, not very cuddly
plastic man
he's a plastic man

Wrapped in rubber he loves to dance.
Sweats inside his plastic pants.
Whips it up into a trance
of Narcissism's withering glance
(in the mirror on the wall
the mirror there sees it all).
A polymer dream that's so inflated,
his love was squashed - and laminated
he's a plastic man
he's a plastic man

You can bend him back but he won't break.
He's a plastic man make no mistake.
Woodworm, mildew, dry-rot, rust,
have no fear of blue-eyed bugs.
Impervious to wear and tear
this man could last for a thousand years!
But just for fun, everyday
he seems to get - thrown away
he's a plastic man
he's a plastic man

Now in years to come, as time goes by,
and archaeologists scratch the veneer of lies,
and everyone needs an oxygen pump,
(in paradise by the rubbish dump)
perhaps they'll wonder upon their knees
who did wrap each slice of cheese?
And say with awe across the land:

Verily it was the plastic man

It's Only Water….

Rain, rain, beautiful rain
why do they hate you so?
With cagoules and drains and glass double-glazed
they try to stem the flow!

Rain. Bountiful rain
the cause of creation to grow
from an earthen corpse to creatures that walk;
why do they hate you so?

From the window bay
of a block of flats
in which I live upstairs
I saw the city awake
in a gorgeous lake
awash with people, prams and chairs.

From far above
I said: 'Let go!
It's only water after all!'
But to the telegraph wire
clung a mother and child
perfectly parallel above the floor…

The water was rising,
the drains were blocked,
cars like boats were sailing away.
I tried to tell them: 'Its only water!'
but: 'Bog off y'bastard!'
was all they could say.

In the blackness above us
the heavens are holy;
as holey as a culinary sieve.
I tried to show them
it's only water
by lapping it up in a plastic lid.

I said: 'Let go!
Me telegraph wire's gonna' snap
with all your weight!'
but like clothes in the wind
on the washing line,
they hung outstretched in the rushing spate.

Across the road where Mrs Thompson lives
the water was rising fast.
It was through the door
and up the stairs,
I saw her banging on the glass.

And then I saw Mr Thompson
bobbing in the surf.
A screaming head above the water
on his way to work.
He seemed to say: 'Uhh..call the Fire Brigaaaaehh...'
in a watery choke,

so I looked around the flooded town
but there wasn't any smoke.
Just Mr Jones, waving madly
as he swept off down the road.
It seems that some are always friendly
despite it being cold.

I chucked them ducks.
I lobbed them loofahs.
I sent them bars of soap.
But every time their faces rose
above the surging water flows
all I heard was: 'Rope...' 'Rope...'

I said: 'Come on! It's only water –
pretend your in the bath!'
But the Amateur Dramatics Society
were getting carried away,
and none of them laughed.

Oh as pretty as the city of Venice - she was
marooned in the morning light.
Suffused in a surge of water
purging the town - not of life
but of all those - who live in bungalows;
and never wanted to know me
until they needed help!

(iv) Psychicbread

The Best and the Worst of Times

Looking forward to a quiet read of the paper, I went for a poo. Only to find David Starkey sitting in the bath plucking a pheasant.

> *Starkey! Starkey! A bright blue little Smartie,*
> *Always has the answer, at any dinner party.*
> *The light he shone in the Moral Maze*
> *Was always hale and hearty.*
> *How I wish we all could be*
> *More like David Starkey!*

On seeing me, he said 'Usually I'll use a pair of pliers but there aren't any in *your* bedroom. However, I'm not here to talk of plucking pheasants. We're living in the best and the worst of times and the worst of it is your poetry. For God's sake stop!' Feeling offended, I slammed the door, then found my tongue and screamed 'No it's not! The worst of it is you, sitting in the bath, plucking a pheasant!' And before he could answer, I covered my ears and hummed like a little boy attempting to terminate Starkey's existence.

And when I looked, he'd gone.

RATS!

There's rats in the cellar.
I tried to get them out
by hurling abuse and a bottle of stout
that smashed on the steps of the cellar stair.
I was watching the tail of a rat disappear.

So I tried to be clever
I tried to be kind
with a trail of sugar to the door outside.
The following day none could be found,
I was Pied Piper of Matlock Town!

And then that night, happily to bed,
under the covers I rightfully said:
'Rats?! Oh, Sugar! Sugar? Rats!'
The place was just a heaving mass
of Rats Sugar Sugar Rats.
I was the candy-man for the big brown rat.

From down in the cellar
up the hall
they follow me to bed when the shadows fall
and fill my mind with devilish dreams,
lurid acts and ugly scenes,
like the one
            where
                    Mrs Thorpe
is bound beneath her husband's Porsche.
And three hours later
he arrives at work
wondering who the hell has tied a lump of ham
to the back of his car...

There's rats in the cellar.
I've got to get them out.
I hear them at noon
when there's no-one about.

They've scratched my scruples,
ripped my clothes.
I thought I might try an overdose
of the purple pellets of coloured poison.
Well Ratus Norvegicus seem to like them.
It makes them quick,
    it makes them strong.
They chased me naked round the lawn.

From behind lace curtains watch
the neighbourhood of Cuthbert's Lodge;
and the following day the doorbell rang.
It was the public health and safety man.
'I understand th'as got Rats!' he said,
without a smile.
I shook my head for quite a while,
as he proceeded to recite with a tireless tongue
Health and Safety – Act I.

By the end of Act II, I could comprehend
this man meant our lease would end
unless I could prove beyond reasonable doubt
that all of the rats had been taken out.

His words they rang like a peal of bells
from glittering towers of principles.
A ceaseless echo throughout the day,
his words were jangling nerves at play:

Oh their whiskers twitch
and their eyes are bright,
bulging with a demon-light.
From out of the sewer they come in droves
to live like freaks in a human home.

In perfect coils their heavy tail
drags behind like a ladies trail.
Their teeth are keen, so too their claws!
Watch them glide across the floor.

All night long, I walked the boards
waiting for the rats, of course.
With a bottle of stout and a fine long knife
I was wearing a wig to perfect a disguise.

Ohhh their whiskers twitch
and their eyes are bright
bulging with a demon light
carried from the dark of sewerage drains
to burn like mad in human brains!

Dressed like a typical farmer's wife
I was cutting off tails with a carving knife.
Did ever you see such a thing in your life?

'Rats!?
　　Naa mate not here, no…

I've got some guinea pigs though.'

Sunlight

Sometimes there is no choice.
Gargoyles clear their throats and sing
in the hallway of our happenings,
in that moment
                    when
the machinery of thought ceases to spin
and instinct is abroad in our corridors of power.

And in that space between our thoughts
leading off to different doors,
in a thousand years who will say
that it mattered anyway
(in the course of time and endless place)
whether George McDower had his hour
and became the president of the United States?

Sometimes there is no choice.
We dare to cross
the stupid comparison drawn in the dust
and walk out in sunlight so strong
our eyes can only meet the ground,
and we walk.

Psychicbread

Bread, bread, psychicbread
nothing quite like it for feeding the head
when its rye bread
        highbred
full of the ergot fungus that bled
meaning
screaming
out of the stone that was really the bone
of his head…. bread

Wake the Dead

If my poems
could wake the dead
I wouldn't bother
reciting them in graveyards,
or over ancient tombs
where the grass grows large.

Nor would I bother
gesticulating
before a funeral hearse,
or upon its bonnet
climb to scrawl
a resuscitating verse. No!

I wouldn't bother.
I'd let the procession pass...

And if my brother
were to suddenly die,
Recite a poem – quick! they'd cry.
And would I? Would I?
                          Would I hell!
No, fly brother, chime that celestial bell.
Go as gentle rain and split the light
into seven shades of which the night is woven.

But if my poems
could wake the dead,
I'd write them on the bridges of the M25
in luminous paint so that day and night
people would stop, leave their cars
and wander over the sidings.

Night and day.
Suddenly *alive* to the whispering grass
and the muffled laughter of clay
pretending to be dead.

(9) Natural History

(v) Natural History

Hideous Reflections

The satirical bard
in the plastic mirror
hung
over the bog:
watches me while
muttering my poems - I
piss into waters that giggle and smile.
Bubble and bounce.

And once I've squeezed
                my every ounce
the bard grins.
O he loves that line
about a prophet who turns:
just water
        into lemon
and lemon
        into lime!

Natural History

They were frightened of freedom
so they caged her with words.
Curious names, like: Moon and Earth.
Snatched from flight
        then gassed and cured,
and fixed like butterflies
        in a collector's drawer.

Synonym, Noun, Adjective, Verb,
arranged on paper
        and pinned at their core.
A masque of what once could bring
our grubs to fly
        on gilded wings.

The Breezeblock Waltz (pt. 2)

Well, I suppose caesium's rhythm
and the revolutions that occur
in a lump of quartz
are measured by your atomic clock,
Mr Briggs.
Yet, failing to recognise how well things work
in their own time, you tell me I'm late.

In daydreams, I have seen my mind
    toiling,
trying to connect
eternal space with mortal flesh, turning
    over and over
the kernel of questions cast by our family tree:
Is the metal of my road a matter of belief?
Our houses built of nothing more than the stuff of…

No. Here on earth, road metal comes from North Uist,
Penmaenmawr, Whatley,
and is laid to the clock of Mr Briggs.

And yet,
in daydreams I have seen my mind
puzzling over the patterns of our flesh.
And try what you will to hide,
we are walking the maze etched upon our fingertips.
Searching for the centre
    where nothing *will* exist…

and houses are built of air.

Brassed Off Billy Monty

The's plenty mek a song n'dance
play the trumpet in the' pants
sing inside an old string vest
wi' rain poundin' cobbled streets
or fillin' up *that* tin bath
to drown the kids or wash the cat
but none can spek o' pain and graft
like our Billy
brassed off Billy
brassed off Billy Monty

And them that ses they've 'ad it tough
sleepin' out
sleepin' rough
sleepin' out's a holiday
when sharin' bed wi' family.

*It's the nicotine stained nostalgia show
the only north you'll ever know
hanging in a photograph*

That's our Billy in the cot
puffin' on his mother's fags.
A dog with mange, uncle Fred
and twenty siblings shared his bed
but deprivation does him good
put some coal dust in his blood
that smoulders in the neighbourhood
of brassed off Billy Monty.

Cos when the town's thro'
and shuttered up
jilted like a £5 slut
and Katy's pregnant before she's 12

and heroin's the only help
and your falling out with your finger nails
as the family turns in on itself
and even your mates are no longer pally
it's time to join the Royal Ballet;
it's time to pray for that 2nd chance
and take to the stage in your underpants:
Come on Billy show us all!
and blow your trumpet at the Albert Hall.
Where the people cheer and bay for more
…more …more
of our Billy
brassed off Billy
brassed off Billy Monty

Wild Garlic

through the sandstone bridge, she said
flows the river Spey
where the wild garlic grows
won't you come and play?

let's play tickle trout, she sighed
whispering like the river
I would I said, *but… can't be late*
back home for me dinner

yet homewards over the mossy wall
she handed me some fruit
a granny smith turning red
at all her talk of juice

all her talk of juice was like
a philtre drunk at bed.
it made me dream a freckled trout
was standing there instead

a freckled trout standing there,
androgynous, divine
singing of the liquid bliss
together we would find

together we would find, she sang
fluttering her gills,
the love that breathes in silver streams,
a love for which you'd kill

a love for which you'd kill - I mused
it filled me full of doubt,
sung beneath the weeping beech
by a brown and greedy trout

a brown and greedy trout, she was
in a sequin dress
that shimmered round her swinging hips
in whisperings of bliss

whisperings of bliss that told
how – on the other side
things are more than they seem
girl   river   trout

the love that hides between the stars

in the light of this

fame and fortune are as nothing;
as wealth made power is as nothing;
as death and hope and desire are
as nothing

in the light of this

the moon is dim,
and the sun is but a ball
of hydrogen. a chemical formula
set on fire

by the light of this

people draw
daydreams on the bathroom wall.
a picture of you opening the fridge
dressed only

in the light of this

we catch a glimpse
of the force that makes the world to spin
and your eyes dance,
like oceans dance

in the light of this

you can read
my thoughts and tell me what they mean.
or slap me hard across the face
and say: *Come round…half-past-eight.*
bring some wine and don't be late.

then in the dark we'll explore
places that we've been before
but never really understood

by the light of this

Pscychicbread CD - Audio

1. The Inevitable Chair (0:55)
2. Helical Staircase (4:08)
3. Alien Rave (5:27)
4. Aunty, Uncle and the Whole Kebab (2:20)
5. Psychicbread (4:25)
6. Season of mists (2:54)
7. Forget (4:01)
8. The Birmingham 666 (0:53)
9. The Best and Worst of Times (1:31)
10. The Art of Eating Aeroplanes (0:42)
11. Orange Girl (3:04)
12. Stop the Week (4:37)
13. Omens in Bloom (4:11)
14. Brassed Off Billy Monty (3:27)
15. Signing Out

Recorded over winter and spring, 2003
at the Foundry Studios, Chesterfield.
All percussive pieces recorded at Deb's and Carl's
and mixed at The Foundry.
Produced by M. G. Jones and Paul Hopkinson.
Percussive pieces arranged by Carl Hodgkinson and M. G. Jones.
Engineered by Paul Hopkinson with assistance
from Mick Twelves and Lee Kerr.

Mark Gwynne Jones and the Whole Kebab are:
Carl Hodgkinson (marimba, udu, Indian drum, sticks)
Deb Rose (djembe, snare, tin-can, pixie-phone, gong, fruit)
Jay Schaffe (conga, high hat, djembe, rain)
Louise Swain (marimba, djembe, cymbal, keys, egg, sticks)
John Thorne (marimba, djembe, snare, sticks)

With special thanks to: Paul for his patience, encouragement and
Alien Rave; Mick for the tanning solution and trips to the library; Lee
for punter's ears, Danny Boy and the Japanese School of Language
and Tom Eckington for a desk to write on.

Pscychicbread CD - Films

1. Mark's Head (00:49)
2. Pickety, Pockety, Poems (00:58)
3. Plasticman (2:38)
4. Alien Love (2:11)
5. It's Only Water (5:00)
6. Possession (7:08)

Mark's Head
Mark Gwynne Jones's head in hideous close-up. (Produced and directed by Andy Lawernce ©1999)

Pickety Pockety Poems
Here we enter the beleaguered mind of a poet and discover that far from being a 'genteel' pastime, poetry is a mad, stalking beast. Verses, words and whisperings won't leave this man alone; they're tapping at the window and banging upstairs' floor. (Produced and directed by Andy Lawrence and Alex Steinitz ©1997)

Plasticman
The tramp of Christmas Future has arrived inside the Superstore. Not to rattle chains, but crackle plastic packaging, frighten fellow shoppers with the horrors of our disposable present and seriously upset the management. (Produced and directed by Andy Lawrence and Alex Steinitz ©1997)

Alien Love
Where does genetic engineering end and weird sex begin? A man on a train declares himself to be a product of Alien Love. An outburst that sees him carried off to an institution; but for who's protection, his or ours? (Produced and directed by Alex Steinitz and M G Jones ©1998)

It's Only Water
Noah lives at the top of a block of flats in Sheffield, and wakes one morning to find it had rained in the night. In fact it had rained quite heavily and the town was flooded. But our hero recognises the need for ablutions and endeavours to persuade those clinging on telegraph wires to Let Go!... It's only water, after all. (Produced and directed by Andy Lawrence and M G Jones ©1999)

Possession
An exploration of dream symbolism and a search for the universal self. This most recent work represents new territory; the intention was to go beyond narrative for this E-motion picture, to create a dream experience rather than attempt to demonstrate meaning. (Produced and directed by Andy Lawrence © 2000)

Contact

To contact Mark Gwynne Jones
email: mark@psychicbread.org

To get up to date information on gigs and other activities visit

www.psychicbread.org

Adult Entertainment

Chloe Poems

ISBN 1 901927 18 0 £6.95

One of the most prodigiously gifted and accessible poets alive today, Chloe Poems has been described as 'an extraordinary mixture of Shirley Temple and pornography.' This collection of political and social commentary, first presented in Midsummer 2002, contains twenty-three poems of uncompromising honesty and explicit republicanism, and comes complete with a fourteen track CD of Chloe live in performance.

Half a Pint of Tristram Shandy

Jo Pearson, Daithidh MacEochaidh, Peter Knaggs

ISBN 1 901927 15 6 £6.95

A three-in-one peotry collection from the best in young poets. Between the leaves of this book lies the mad boundless energy of the globe cracking-up under our very noses; it is a world which is harnessed in images of jazz, sex, drugs, aliens, abuse; in effective colloquial language and manic syntax; but the themes are always treated with gravity, unsettling candour and humour.

I Am

Michelle Scally-Clarke

ISBN 1 901927 08 3 £10 Including free CD

At thirty years old, Michelle is the same age as the mother who gave her up into care as a baby. In the quest to find her birth parents, her roots and her own identity, this book traces the journey from care, to adoption, to motherhood, to performer. Using the fragments of her own memory, her poetry and extracts from her adoption files, Michelle rebuilds the picture of 'self' that allows her to transcend adversity and move forward to become the woman she was born to be.

You can hear the beat and song of Michelle Scally-Clarke on the CD that accompanies this book and, on the inside pages, read the story that is the source of that song.

Moveable Type
Rommi Smith
ISBN 1 901927 11 3 £10 Including free CD

It is the theme of discovery that is at the heart of *Moveable Type*. Rommi Smith takes the reader on a journey through identity, language and memory, via England and America, with sharp observation, wit and wry comment en route. The insights and revelations invite us not only to look beneath the surface of the places we live in, but also ourselves. *Moveable Type* and its accompanying CD offer the reader the opportunity to listen or read, read and listen. Either way, you are witnessing a sound that is uniquely Rommi Smith.

Other Titles From Route - Fiction

Next Stop Hope - *route 14*
Eds M Y Alam, Anthony Cropper, Ian Daley
ISBN 1-901927 19 9 £6.95

The latest title in the route series, this bumper issue brings together further chronicles of contemporary preoccupations. Presented in three distinct collections: *Criminally Minded, Something Has Gone Wrong In The World* and *Next Stop Hope* – this anthology of new writing takes you skilfully through the inner workings of the criminal mind, the nuances of human relationships and our personal connections with an increasingly disturbing world, where hope is hard to find.

Featuring new short fiction and poetry from thirty-three writers including M Y Alam, Val Cale, Anthony Cropper, Susan Everett, Mark Gwynne Jones, Daithidh MacEochaidh, Jo Pearson, Chloe Poems, Michelle Scally-Clarke and Adrian Wilson.

Warehouse
MS Green, Alan Green, Clayton Devanny,
Simon Nodder, Jono Bell - Ed Ian Daley
ISBN 1-901927 10 5 £6.95

Warehouse is a unique type of social realism, written by young warehouse operatives from the bottom end of the labour market in the middle of the post-industrial heartland, it steps to the beat of modern day working-class life. A soundtrack to the stories is included on a complimentary CD, warehouse blues supplied by *The Chapter* and urban funk grooves from *Budists*

One Northern Soul
J R Endeacott
ISBN 1-901927 17 2 £6.95

If that goal in Paris had been allowed then everything that followed could have been different. For young Stephen Bottomley something died that night. One Northern Soul follows the fortunes of this Leeds United fan as he comes of age in the dark days of the early eighties with no prospects, no guidance and to cap it all, his beloved football team suffer relegation to the Second Division.

This book is a reminder of a recent past and of connected fates. J R Endeacott has drawn a story that captures the mood of a time and a place, bottling the atmosphere of the terrace in its final days as disaster was about to strike and bring about wholesale and lasting change.

Kilo
M Y Alam
ISBN 1-901927 09 1 £6.95

Khalil Khan was a good boy. He had a certain past and an equally certain future awaited until gangsters decided to turn his world upside down. They shattered his safe family life with baseball bats but that's just the beginning. They turned good, innocent and honest Khalil into someone else: Kilo, a much more unforgiving and determined piece of work. Kilo cuts his way through the underworld of Bradford street crime, but the closer he gets to the top of that game, the stronger the pull of his original values become. When he finally begins to rub shoulders with the men who inadvertently showed him the allure of crime, the more convinced he becomes that it is sometimes necessary to bad in order to achieve good.

'M Y Alam consistently articulates the experience of dual cultural identity, of being British born with Pakistani heritage and he violently runs this through the mixer with life on the mean streets seasoned with references to hip-hop and American gangster movies.'

The Blackstuff
Val Cale
ISBN 1-901927 14 8 £6.95

'The mind is like a creamy pint of Guinness…The head is the engine that drives you through the day…the fuel however lies in the blackstuff, in the darkness, in the depths of the unexplored cave which is your subconscious mind…this is the story of my journey through the blackstuff.'

The Blackstuff is a true story of a road-trip that sees Val Cale in trouble in Japan, impaled in Nepal, ripped off at a vaginal freak show in Bangkok, nearly saturated by a masturbating Himalayan bear in the most southerly town of India and culminates in a mad tramp across the world looking for the ultimate blowjob and the meaning of life.

The Blackstuff is *not* just a book. It is *not* just the opinion of an individual who feels that he has something important to say. This is a story which every last one of us can relate to, a story about the incessant battle between our internal angels and our demented demons. This is an odyssey to the liquefied centre of the brain, a magic carpet ride surfing on grass and pills, seas of booze, and the enormous strength of the human soul.

The Blackstuff takes you beyond the beach, deeper into the ocean of darkness that is the pint of stout in your head...

Weatherman

Anthony Cropper

ISBN 1-901927 16 4 £6.95

Ken sits out the back, in the flatlands that surround Old Goole, and watches the weather. That's what he was doing with poor Lucy, that fateful day, sat on the roof of his house, lifting her up to the sky. Lucy's friend, Florrie, she knew what would happen.

All this is picked up by Alfie de Losinge's machine, which he had designed to control the weather. Instead, amongst the tiny atoms of cloud formations, he receives fragmentary images of events that slowly unfold to reveal a tender, and ultimately tragic, love story.

In this beautifully crafted first novel, Anthony Cropper skilfully draws a picture of life inextricably linked to the environment, the elements, and the ever changing weather.

Very Acme

Adrian Wilson

ISBN: 1 901927 12 1 £6.95

New Nomad, nappy expert, small town man and ultimately a hologram – these are the life roles of Adrian Wilson, hero and author of this book, which when he began writing it, was to become the world's first novel about two and a half streets. He figured that all you ever needed to know could be discovered within a square mile of his room, an easy claim to make by a man who's family hadn't moved an inch in nearly seven centuries. All this changes when a new job sends him all around the world, stories of Slaughter and the Dogs and Acme Terrace give way to Procter and Gamble and the Russian Mafia. He starts feeling nostalgic for the beginning of the book before he gets to the end.

Very Acme is two books within one, it is about small town life in the global age and trying to keep a sense of identity in a world of multi-corporations and information overload.

Like A Dog To Its Vomit
Daithidh MacEochaidh
ISBN: 1 901927 07 5 £6.95

Somewhere between the text, the intertext and the testosterone find Ron Smith, illiterate book lover, philosopher of non-thought and the head honcho's left-arm man. Watch Ron as he oversees the begging franchise on Gunnarsgate, shares a room with a mouse of the Lacota Sioux and makes love to Tracy back from the dead and still eager to get into his dungarees. There's a virgin giving birth under the stairs, putsch at the taxi rank and Kali, Goddess of Death, is calling. Only Arturo can sort it, but Arturo is travelling. In part two find out how to live in a sock and select sweets from a shop that time forgot and meet a no-holds barred state registered girlfriend. In part three, an author promises truth, but the author is dead - isn't she?

In this complex, stylish and downright dirty novel, Daithidh MacEochaidh belts through underclass underachieving, postponed-modern sacrilege and the more pungent bodily orifices.

Crazy Horse
Susan Everett
ISBN 1 901927 06 7 £6.95

Jenny Barker, like many young women, has a few problems. She is trying to get on with her life, but it isn't easy. She was once buried underneath the sand and it had stopped her growing up, plus she had killed the milkman. Her beloved horse has been stolen while the vicious *Savager* is on the loose cutting up animals in fields. She's neither doing well in college nor in love and fears she may die a virgin.

Crazy Horse is a wacky ride.

The Route Series

*An important aspect of route is to keep work fresh, of its time
and highly visible. The route series is a valuable tool to achieve
that aim. A combination of commisions and submissions,
mixing short fiction with poetry and articles from an assortment
of writers. The first thirteen issues were newspapers.*

For online content and to purchase
back issues please visit

www.route-online.com

Route Subscription

Route's subscription scheme is the easiest way for readers to keep in touch with new work from the best of new writers. Subscribers receive a minimum of four books per year, which could take the form of a novel, an anthology of short stories, a novella, a poetry collection or an issue in the route series. Any additional publications and future issues of the route paper will also be mailed direct to subscribers, as well as information on route events and digital projects.

Route constantly strives to promote the best in under represented voices, outside of the mainstream, and will give support to develop promising new talent. By subscribing to route, you too will be supporting these artists.

The fee is modest.

UK £15
Europe £20 (35• approx)
Rest of World £25(US$40 approx)

Subscribe online now at www.route-online.com

To receive a postal subscription form email your details to books@route-online.com or send your details to:
route, school lane, glasshoughton, wf10 4qh, uk

Psychicbread is a title on the route subscription scheme.